I0458587

TEACHING
ON LOW FUEL
From A Christian Perspective

ANTHONY DAYSE, PH.D.

Copyright © 2025 Anthony Dayse. All rights reserved. No part of this publication may be reproduced, distributed, or transmitted in any form or by any means, including photocopying, recording, or other electronic or mechanical methods, without the prior written permission of the publisher, except in the case of brief quotations embodied in critical reviews and certain other noncommercial uses permitted by copyright law. For permission requests, write to the publisher, addressed "Attention: Permissions Coordinator," at the address below.

ISBN: 978-1-965082-30-0

Publishing By: DemiCo National, LLC

www.DemiCoNational.com

CHAPTERS-AT-LARGE

Preface   Page 8

1. The Daily Struggles of Teaching   Page 10

2. Finding Spiritual Renewal   Page 39

3. Building Resilience   Page 65

4. Navigating Challenges   Page 81

5. Community Support   Page 91

6. Personal Growth   Page 96

7. Integration of Faith and Teaching   Page 104

8. Finding Purpose   Page 112

Chapter Overview

Chapter 1.

The Daily Struggles of Teaching deals with Exploring the demanding nature of teaching and the toll it can take on teachers' mental, emotional, and physical well-being.

Chapter 2.

Finding Spiritual Renewal discusses how teachers can find solace and renewal through their faith, especially during times of stress and burnout.

Chapter 3.

Building Resilience offers strategies for building resilience through spiritual practices, such as prayer, meditation, and reflection.

Chapter 4.

Navigating Challenges provides practical advice for navigating common challenges in the classroom, such as difficult students, parent interactions, and administrative pressures, with a spiritual perspective.

Chapter 5.

Community Support stresses the importance of community and support networks within the teaching profession, and how these connections can be strengthened through faith.

Chapter 6.

Personal Growth encourages all to have personal growth and self-care practices that align with spiritual principles, emphasizing the importance of prioritizing one's well-being.

Chapter 7.

Integration of Faith and Teaching discusses how teachers can integrate their faith into their teaching practice, creating a more holistic and meaningful experience for both them and their students.

Chapter 8.

Finding Purpose helps teachers rediscover their sense of purpose and passion for teaching by connecting it to their spiritual beliefs and values.

Preface

Teaching is a labor of love, but it can also be incredibly challenging. As a teacher, you pour your heart and soul into your work, facing daily struggles and complexities that can leave you feeling drained and overwhelmed. You look forward to the weekend for a much-needed break, only to find that even time with loved ones you can't fully recharge your spirit.

Have you ever experienced that moment in church when you felt a surge of hope, a glimpse of relief from your burdens? You pray, you cry, you feel a sense of breakthrough. But as you leave the sanctuary, reality hits you like a ton of bricks – you're back to square one, facing the same challenges and uncertainties before stepping into the church.

In this book, Dr. Dayse takes you on a journey through the unique challenges that Christian teachers face in balancing their professional and personal lives. Whether you're a seasoned educator or just starting out, this book offers insights and guidance to help you navigate the complexities of teaching from a spiritual perspective.

Are you ready to embark on this journey? For some, it will be a new experience, a fresh perspective on the intersection of faith and teaching. For others, it will feel like déjà vu, a familiar yet enlightening path to rediscovering the joy and purpose in your work.

Through personal anecdotes, practical advice, and deep spiritual insights, Dr. Dayse will show you how developing a strong relationship with God can sustain you in your role as a teacher. You'll learn how to build your full armor, strengthening your faith and resilience in the face of adversity.

Join Dr. Dayse as he guides you through the challenges and triumphs of teaching on low fuel, offering a roadmap to spiritual renewal and professional fulfillment.

Chapter 1: The Daily Struggles of Teaching

Addressing the daily struggles of teaching requires us to confront the profound challenges educators face, including the immense pressure that can impact their mental, emotional, and physical health. Reflecting on these challenges, I recall an article I wrote years ago titled 'The Love of Teaching Won't Pay the Rent.' This sentiment rings true, as educators often find themselves balancing the noble act of teaching with the harsh realities of financial strain. It's disheartening when the very act of sharing knowledge is hindered by personal financial struggles. Many educators, while relying on their faith for strength, may feel overwhelmed. As my mother would say, during moments of deep trouble, 'look to the hills, from where your help will come.'

Daily life as a teacher is often a delicate balancing act, requiring them to navigate a multitude of challenges while maintaining a positive outlook. Imagine starting your day with a heavy heart, weighed down by the strains of a difficult relationship or the looming threat of financial insecurity. For many educators, these are not hypothetical scenarios but harsh realities they confront each day. According to a recent survey, worldwide, stress and burnout continue to be a problem among teachers, leading to anxiety and depression ([NCBI, 2022]). Burnout may adversely affect teachers' health and is a risk factor for poor physical and mental well-being. Determining the prevalence and correlates of stress, burnout, anxiety, and depression among teachers is essential for addressing this public health concern. When faced with such challenges, teachers often find solace in their faith, relying on the strength they draw from spiritual beliefs to persevere. However, the stress of unpaid bills, the fear of utility disconnections, and the constant pressure of making ends meet on a meager salary can take a significant toll, threatening to break even the most resilient spirit.

Teaching Impacts Teachers' Mental, Emotional, and Physical Well-Being

The pressure of teaching has a profound impact on teachers' mental, emotional, and physical well-being. It can cause even the best educators to struggle to function at their best, leading to decreased performance compared to what they would achieve under normal circumstances. This decline in performance not only affects teachers but also impacts the morale of other teachers, staff, and students.

The mental and emotional strain of teaching pressure can be overwhelming, affecting teachers' ability to focus, make decisions, and engage effectively with students. This, in turn, can hinder the learning process and impact the quality of education students receive. Moreover, the constant stress and pressure can lead to burnout, a state of emotional, physical, and mental exhaustion that can have long-lasting effects on teachers' well-being.

From a spiritual perspective, the pressure of teaching can be viewed as a spiritual attack, as it undermines teachers' ability to fulfill their calling and serve as effective educators. This attack on their mental, emotional, and physical well-being can leave teachers feeling drained, discouraged, and disconnected from their purpose.

In conclusion, the pressure of teaching is not just a professional challenge but also a deeply personal and spiritual one. It affects all aspects of the teaching profession and requires teachers to find ways to protect their well-being and maintain their passion for teaching despite the challenges they face.

Financial Challenges that Educators Often Encounter

If you are about to be evicted from your apartment or your mortgage is overdue or because of non-payment or your utility bill has been disconnected, this can be a serious challenge. Many teachers enter the profession out of a deep love for education and a desire to make a difference in students' lives. However, when they are struggling to pay rent, keep the lights on, or afford the basic necessities, and their financial burdens can significantly impact their ability to teach effectively.

When an educator is constantly worried about eviction, overdue bills, or even affording gas to get to work, their focus is split between survival and teaching. This financial strain can lead to stress, exhaustion, and burnout, making it difficult to bring the energy, patience, and creativity needed to engage students.

Additionally, low salaries often force teachers to take on second or even third jobs, leaving them with less time to prepare lessons, grade assignments, or invest in professional development. Some teachers also spend their own money on classroom supplies, further stretching their already limited budgets.

The financial challenges educators face are not just personal issues, they affect the entire learning environment. A stressed, overworked, and financially struggling teacher cannot give their best to students. If we truly value education, we must ensure that teachers are paid a livable wage so they can focus on what they do best: teaching and shaping the future.

Additional Financial Challenges Educators Face:

Low Salaries and Inadequate Compensation:

Many teachers earn salaries that do not adequately compensate for their level of education, experience, and workload. This often forces educators to take on second jobs or side gigs to make ends meet, leading to increased stress and less time for classroom preparation.

Out-of-Pocket Expenses:

Like most teachers, I have spent my own money on classroom supplies, educational materials, and even snacks for students. I know this can strain one's personal finances and add to the financial burdens.

Lack of Benefits and Support:

Inadequate health insurance, retirement plans, and other benefits can make financial planning difficult for teachers, contributing to long-term financial insecurity.

Student Loan Debt:

Many educators have significant student loan debt from obtaining their degrees and certifications. High monthly payments can make it challenging to save or invest in their future.

Cost of Continuing Education:

As teachers, we are often required to pursue continuing education to maintain our certifications or advance in our careers. These courses and workshops can be costly and time-consuming.

Impact on Teaching Effectiveness

Increased Stress and Burnout:

Financial stress can lead to burnout, affecting a teachers' mental and emotional health. Burnout can diminish their enthusiasm, patience, and energy levels, making it harder to engage and inspire students.

Reduced Focus and Productivity:

From firsthand experience, worrying about financial issues can distract you from your primary responsibilities, reducing your ability to plan effective lessons, grade assignments promptly, and provide individual attention to students.

Decreased Job Satisfaction:

Persistent financial difficulties can lead to decreased job satisfaction and a sense of frustration or helplessness, potentially increasing turnover rates among educators.

Negative Impact on Classroom Environment:

Financial stress can influence a teacher's mood and interactions with students, potentially creating a less supportive and positive learning environment.

Spiritual Guidance for Financial Challenges

I encourage teachers to seek comfort and direction through prayer. Finding quiet moments to connect with your faith can provide peace and clarity amid financial turmoil.

Building a Support Network:

I suggest forming or joining support groups with fellow educators who understand your struggles. Sharing experiences and advice can foster a sense of community and solidarity.

Practicing Gratitude:

Emphasize the importance of gratitude for what you have, even in difficult times. Focusing on positive aspects of your life and career can help shift your perspective even when you are at your lowest.

Trusting in God's Provision:

I encourage you to trust that your needs will be met, even when the situation seems dire. Believing in God's provision can offer hope and reduce anxiety about the future.

Financial Stewardship and Planning:

Seeking practical advice on budgeting, saving, and managing expenses will not hurt. I suggest resources like financial counseling or workshops to help gain better control over your finances.

Seeking Professional Help:

Let's not forget professional financial advice or counseling. Sometimes, an outside perspective can provide new insights and solutions to financial problems.

Balancing the Noble Aspects of Teaching

Balancing the noble calling of teaching with the harsh realities of financial strain requires deep faith and trust in God's provision. Educators who struggle to make ends meet often lean on their spiritual foundation to find strength, wisdom, and endurance. Prayer becomes a lifeline, offering peace in moments of uncertainty and clarity in times of decision-making. Through prayer, teachers seek not only financial relief but also guidance on managing their resources wisely and trusting that their needs will be met.

Reading scripture provides comfort and perspective. Biblical teachings remind educators that while financial struggles are real, they do not define their worth or the impact of their work. Verses like Philippians 4:19 ("And my God will supply every need of yours according to His riches in glory in Christ Jesus") offer reassurance that God sees their struggles and will provide in His time. Scripture also calls for wise stewardship, encouraging educators to reflect on spending habits, seek financial wisdom, and trust God's direction in overcoming challenges.

Additionally, faith-based communities play a crucial role in supporting educators. Seeking counsel from ministers, joining prayer groups, and surrounding themselves with believers who uplift and encourage them can bring both spiritual and practical solutions. These connections can open doors to opportunities, whether through financial assistance, job advice, or simply the strength to persevere in their calling.

Ultimately, balancing the joys of teaching with financial hardship requires surrendering to God's plan while taking practical steps to improve one's situation. Educators walk by faith, knowing that their work has a divine purpose and that their sacrifices are not in vain. Through prayer, scripture, and community, they find the resilience to continue shaping young lives, even in the face of financial struggles.

Therefore, balancing the noble calling of teaching with the harsh realities of financial strain is a challenge that many educators face, but faith provides strength, perspective, and hope. Because we know teaching is more than just a profession—it is a calling, a ministry of service, and an act of love. However, when financial hardships arise, it can be difficult to stay focused on this higher purpose. In these moments, educators turn to God for guidance, strength, and provision.

Turning to Prayer for Strength and Direction

Prayer is not just a request for financial relief; it is a means of finding peace amid uncertainty. When financial burdens become overwhelming—when rent is due, when the bank account is empty, when the weight of providing for one's family feels too heavy—prayer serves as a source of refuge. Matthew 11:28 reminds us, "Come to me, all you who are weary and burdened, and I will give you rest." Teachers often carry not only their own worries but also the struggles of their students, making it essential to surrender their burdens to God through prayer.

Many educators form prayer circles or seek out prayer warriors who intercede on their behalf. These faith-based support systems not only bring comfort but also encourage accountability in making wise financial and spiritual decisions. Seeking God's wisdom in financial matters helps teachers approach their struggles with faith rather than fear. James 1:5 assures us, "If any of you lacks wisdom, you should ask God, who gives generously to all without finding fault, and it will be given to you."

Finding Guidance in Scripture

Reading scripture provides reassurance that God is both aware of and concerned about financial hardships. Philippians 4:19 declares, "And my God will supply every need of yours according to his riches in glory in Christ Jesus." This promise serves as a reminder that, even in times of struggle, God provides in ways that may not always be immediate or expected.

The Bible also teaches about financial stewardship. Educators who struggle financially may reflect on how their spending habits align with biblical principles. Proverbs 21:5 states, "The plans of the diligent lead surely to abundance, but everyone who is hasty comes only to poverty." Seeking wisdom in financial planning, avoiding unnecessary debt, and trusting God's timing can be powerful steps toward financial stability.

Seeking Strength Through Community and Ministry

Educators do not have to walk through financial hardship alone. The body of Christ is meant to uplift and encourage one another. Many teachers turn to their ministers for spiritual guidance or connect with church groups that offer financial counseling, assistance, or job-related opportunities. Hebrews 10:24-25 reminds us, "And let us consider how we may spur one another on toward love and good deeds, not giving up meeting together, as some are in the habit of doing, but encouraging one another."

The emotional toll of financial stress can be heavy, and without a strong support system, it can lead to burnout. Having a faith-based community allows teachers to not only receive help but also to be reminded of their value and purpose beyond their paycheck.

A Personal Reflection

I've heard stories of educators who, despite financial hardship, continued to trust God's provision—and He showed up in unexpected ways. One teacher shared how she was down to her last few dollars, not knowing how she would buy groceries, only to receive an unexpected blessing from a church member who felt led to help her. Another teacher, struggling to pay rent, was offered an additional tutoring opportunity that provided just enough income to cover her needs. These testimonies serve as reminders that God is faithful, even when we do not see immediate answers.

As educators, it's easy to feel disheartened by the financial challenges that come with the profession. However, trusting in God's provision, practicing wise stewardship, and leaning on a faith-filled community can help teachers stay encouraged. Teaching may not always provide financial wealth, but its impact is eternal. As Galatians 6:9 reminds us, "Let us not grow weary in doing good, for at the proper time we will reap a harvest if we do not give up."

Through prayer, scripture, and community, teachers can find the balance between the noble calling of education and the financial realities they face, knowing that God sees, cares, and will provide in His perfect timing.

The role faith plays in helping educators cope with challenges

Faith plays a tremendous role in everything we do, especially in the lives of educators. Every day, teachers walk into situations unknown to them, encountering students with unique struggles, bureaucratic pressures, and financial hardships. Although we know that the calling to teach is real, we must also acknowledge that the spiritual battles in this profession are just as real. The weight of these challenges can sometimes feel unbearable, tempting educators to throw in the towel and say, "Enough!"

This is where faith—and God's unchanging hands—becomes a lifeline. The trials that teachers face often make them feel as though they are pouring from an empty cup. The exhaustion, the feeling of being undervalued, and the financial struggles can create a deep sense of emptiness, as though there is nothing left to offer beyond the calling itself. Yet, it is in these moments that faith reminds us that we are never alone. Isaiah 41:10 reassures us: "Fear not, for I am with you; be not dismayed, for I am your God; I will strengthen you, I will help you, I will uphold you with my righteous right hand."

Faith gives educators the strength to persevere, not because the journey is easy, but because they trust that God walks beside them. When the burden becomes too heavy, faith teaches them to surrender it to the One who carries all burdens. Matthew 11:28 echoes this promise: "Come to me, all who labor and are heavy laden, and I will give you rest."

The Power of Worship in Times of Struggle

This reminds me of the timeless hymn Rock of Ages. The lyrics, "Rock of Ages, cleft for me, let me hide myself in Thee," speak to the deep need for refuge in God. Educators, like all who serve in difficult roles, sometimes need a place to hide—a place to rest in the assurance that

God is their shelter, their strong foundation, their unshakable rock. When the world offers no solutions, faith provides a place of safety where they can find renewal and strength.

Worship, whether through song, scripture, or prayer, shifts the focus from the problem to the Provider. When educators face days where they feel unseen, undervalued, or drained, worship reminds them that their work is not in vain. 1 Corinthians 15:58 encourages: "Therefore, my dear brothers and sisters, stand firm. Let nothing move you. Always give yourselves fully to the work of the Lord, because you know that your labor in the Lord is not in vain."

Faith as the Source of Strength and Endurance

Faith doesn't remove the challenges, but it gives teachers the endurance to press on. It allows them to see beyond the struggles of today and trust that God is working all things together for good. Romans 8:28 reminds us: "And we know that in all things God works for the good of those who love Him, who have been called according to His purpose." Even when the road is difficult, faith teaches educators to believe that their sacrifices are part of a greater plan—one that shapes not only their own lives but the lives of every student they touch.

At the end of the day, faith sustains educators because it keeps their eyes on the One who called them to this work. It reminds them that their strength does not come from their own abilities, but from God's unwavering presence in their lives. When they feel like they have nothing left to give, faith whispers, "Be still and know that I am God." (Psalm 46:10)

Through prayer, worship, scripture, and trust in God's provision, educators find the strength to continue, knowing that they are held by His unchanging hands.

Finding Support and Resources to Help Navigate The Difficulties of Teaching

Educators can find support and resources to help them navigate the difficulties of teaching by leaning on their faith and seeking out a community of like-minded believers who understand the spiritual and emotional demands of the profession. Teaching can often feel like a solitary journey, but God never intended for us to walk alone. Proverbs 27:17 reminds us, "As iron sharpens iron, so one person sharpens another." When educators connect with fellow teachers who love God and share their commitment to both their students and their faith, they find strength, encouragement, and renewed purpose.

The Power of Fellowship and Prayer

One of the greatest sources of support is the power of prayer and Christian fellowship. Teachers who surround themselves with a community of believers—whether through a church group, a Bible study, or a circle of faith-filled colleagues—can find reassurance in knowing that others are praying for them. Matthew 18:20 reminds us, "For where two or three gather in my name, there am I with them." When educators come together in prayer, they invite God's presence into their struggles, seeking His wisdom and peace in moments of uncertainty.

Educators can also turn to spiritual mentors—ministers, pastors, or seasoned Christian teachers—who can provide godly counsel and help them navigate their challenges with biblical wisdom. Just as Moses relied on Aaron and Hur to lift his arms when he grew weary in battle (Exodus 17:12), teachers need those who will lift them up when the burdens of the profession feel too heavy to bear alone.

God as The Ultimate Provider of Resources

While seeking external resources is important, educators must also remember that God is the ultimate provider of wisdom, strength, and provision. Philippians 4:19 assures us, "And my God will supply every need of yours according to His riches in glory in Christ Jesus."

When financial strain, emotional exhaustion, or feelings of inadequacy arise, educators can trust that God will open doors—whether through unexpected opportunities, financial provision, or the right words at the right time.

Practical Steps in Seeking Support

In addition to spiritual resources, educators can also find strength and guidance through:

Faith-Based Teacher Organizations– Groups that provide spiritual encouragement and practical resources for educators facing challenges.

Church-Based Support Groups– Many churches have ministries dedicated to professionals, including educators, offering mentorship and prayer support.

Scripture and Devotional Study– Daily meditation on God's Word provides encouragement and insight, helping teachers remain grounded in their faith. Isaiah 40:31 reminds us, "But those who hope in the Lord will renew their strength."

Sabbath and Rest in God– Teachers often give so much of themselves that they neglect rest. God commands us to rest in Him, trusting that He will sustain us. Exodus 33:14 says, "My presence will go with you, and I will give you rest."

Ultimately, when educators seek the right support, God will direct their path. By turning to Him first, He will lead them to the people, resources, and opportunities that will strengthen them for the road ahead.

Strategies Educators Use to Maintain Their Mental, Emotional, and Physical Health

Educators face immense mental, emotional, and physical challenges in their profession, but through faith, they can develop strategies to maintain their well-being and continue their calling with strength.

The key is to establish a strong spiritual foundation, relying on God as the ultimate source of renewal. Isaiah 40:31 reminds us, "But those who hope in the Lord will renew their strength. They will soar on wings like eagles; they will run and not grow weary, they will walk and not faint."

1. *Establishing a Faith-Based Support System*

No teacher should walk alone. Surrounding oneself with a community of believers—whether fellow teachers, church members, or prayer warriors—helps to provide encouragement, accountability, and intercession during difficult times. Ecclesiastes 4:9-10 states, "Two are better than one, because they have a good return for their labor: If either of them falls down, one can help the other up." A strong support system acts as a lifeline when the burdens of teaching become too heavy.

2. *The Power of Prayer and Spiritual Armor*

Prayer is a direct line to God, offering peace in the midst of chaos. Educators should cultivate a habit of daily prayer, seeking God's wisdom, patience, and strength before stepping into the classroom. Additionally, wearing the full armor of God, as described in Ephesians 6:10-18, is crucial. Teaching is not just a profession, it is a battlefield where educators must stand firm against discouragement, fatigue, and spiritual attacks. By putting on the armor of God—truth, righteousness, faith, salvation, and the Word—they can face every challenge with confidence.

3. *Meditating on Scripture for Strength*

Just as fuel keeps a car running, the Word of God sustains weary educators. Keeping key scriptures on hand—written on sticky notes, saved on a phone, or recited in moments of stress—provides instant encouragement. Some powerful verses include:

Philippians 4:13– "I can do all things through Christ who strengthens me."

Psalm 46:1– "God is our refuge and strength, a very present help in trouble."

2 Corinthians 12:9– "My grace is sufficient for you, for my power is made perfect in weakness."

4. *Physical and Emotional Self-Care Rooted in Faith*

Even Jesus took time to rest and recharge. Educators must recognize that self-care is not selfish—it is necessary to fulfill their God-given calling. Setting aside time for Sabbath rest (Exodus 20:8-10) allows teachers to reset spiritually, mentally, and physically.

Other essential self-care strategies include:

Exercise and proper nutrition– Honoring God by taking care of the body He has given us. (1 Corinthians 6:19-20)

Journaling and reflection– Writing down prayers and victories to see how God is moving.

Worship and music– Uplifting songs like "Rock of Ages" or "It Is Well With My Soul" bring peace in times of distress.

5. *Confidence in God as the Provider*

When finances are tight, when exhaustion sets in, or when discouragement creeps in, educators must stand firm in the promise that God is our provider. Matthew 6:31-33 reminds us not to worry about our needs but to seek God first, and He will take care of the rest. Trusting in His provision allows educators to remain focused on their mission without being overwhelmed by fear.

Refueling for The Journey

When the fuel runs low, educators must return to their source—God. With prayer, scripture, faith, and a strong support system, they can refill their spiritual tank and continue their mission with renewed strength. Galatians 6:9 encourages, "Let us not grow weary in doing good, for at the proper time we will reap a harvest if we do not give up."

Schools and Communities Can Better Support Teachers

As schools know morale of teachers depreciates as the year goes by, Administrators know teachers experience "teaching on low fuel." This is a real experience. Having a strong relationship with God can be hard, but a Spiritual connection helps because there's a scripture that says you only have the faith the size of a mustard seed, because teaching is not just a job; it is a calling. Yet, the weight of daily struggles—low pay, exhaustion, and emotional burnout—can leave educators feeling depleted.

Schools and communities have a responsibility to recognize these struggles and provide meaningful support. Just as educators pour into the lives of students, they need to be refilled—mentally, emotionally, and spiritually.

1. *Recognizing and Addressing Teacher Morale*

Schools must acknowledge that teacher morale depreciates throughout the year. The enthusiasm of August often fades by December, and by spring, many teachers are barely holding on. This is why intentional efforts should be made to uplift educators, reinforcing the spiritual truth found in Galatians 6:9: "Let us not grow weary in doing good, for at the proper time we will reap a harvest if we do not give up."

Schools should create spaces for prayer and reflection– Offering optional morning devotions, prayer groups, or quiet spaces for reflection can help teachers stay spiritually connected.

Community organizations can adopt teachers– Churches and faith-based organizations can sponsor teachers by providing small acts of kindness, prayer partnerships, or financial assistance for classroom supplies.

Encourage faith-based mentorship– Pairing seasoned teachers with newer educators in spiritually grounded mentorship relationships can reinforce a sense of purpose and encouragement.

2. *The Power of Faith: A Mustard Seed is Enough*

Jesus teaches in Matthew 17:20, "If you have faith as small as a mustard seed, you can say to this mountain, 'Move from here to there,' and it will move." Many teachers feel overwhelmed, believing they don't have enough strength to keep going. However, faith—even a small amount—can sustain them through the toughest days. Schools and communities can:

> You should hold onto small victories. Administrators and colleagues should recognize your' efforts, no matter how small, reminding them that God sees your work.

> Create a culture of gratitude and encouragement. Words of affirmation, thank-you notes, and community appreciation events can remind educators that their work is valued.

3. *Providing Physical and Emotional Support*

Even Jesus took time to rest and retreat. Schools should prioritize teacher well-being by implementing policies that prevent burnout, such as:

Mental health days and flexible support– Just as students need emotional support, teachers do too. Schools should provide access to counseling, peer support groups, and wellness initiatives.

Community outreach programs– Local churches and organizations can host events such as teacher appreciation luncheons, supply drives, or financial aid programs to help struggling educators.

4. *Strengthening the Connection Between Schools, Churches, and the Community*

Faith communities play a crucial role in uplifting teachers. Proverbs 11:25 states, "A generous person will prosper; whoever refreshes others will be refreshed." When communities pour into teachers, they, in turn, pour into students.

Faith-based organizations can offer prayer support, sending encouraging scriptures or organizing prayer circles for teachers. Local businesses can assist with financial relief, offering teacher discounts or sponsorship programs for classroom needs.

Churches can host teacher appreciation services, acknowledging the spiritual warfare that comes with the profession and covering teachers in prayer.

5. *Restoring Purpose and Calling*

Trust me, it is easy to forget your divine calling when overwhelmed by struggles. Although this does not happen often enough, schools and communities should remind teachers that they are not just employees—they are shaping lives. Colossians 3:23 encourages, "Whatever you do, work at it with all your heart, as working for the Lord, not for human masters."

Administrators should foster a supportive leadership style that acknowledges teachers' struggles and offers solutions rooted in empathy and faith. Communities should help teachers find balance by encouraging them to take time for worship, personal devotion, and rest.

Rebuilding Teachers, One Prayer at a Time

You are on the battlefield daily, often feeling drained and unappreciated. However, with the right spiritual, emotional, and practical support, you can continue your mission with faith as your fuel. Schools and communities must work together to pour back into teachers, strengthening their spirits so they can continue shaping the future with passion and purpose.

<u>Reflecting</u>

When I reflect on my journey as an educator, I will always remember the struggles I had—financially, emotionally, and spiritually. I know what it is like to wake up in the morning, put on a brave face, and walk into a classroom full of students while silently battling worries that weigh heavy on my heart. Smiling through the storm, I would teach lessons with passion, all while wondering how I would pay my bills, keep the lights on, or even find the strength to keep going.

I recall nights of crying out to Jesus, not just out of habit, but out of desperation. Psalm 46:1 tells us, "God is our refuge and strength, an ever-present help in trouble." There were days when I questioned my calling, wondering, "Lord, if You have called me to this work, why is it so hard?" But that is when I learned that faith is not about avoiding the storm; it is about trusting God in the storm. I remember a particularly difficult time when my financial struggles felt unbearable. I had exhausted all my resources, and the burden was heavy. One evening, I sat alone, praying, "Lord, I don't know how I will make it, but I know You are Jehovah Jireh—my provider."

That night, I opened my Bible and landed on Matthew 6:26, which says, "Look at the birds of the air; they do not sow or reap or store away in barns, and yet your Heavenly Father feeds them. Are you not much more valuable than them?" It was a reminder that my struggles were not unseen. God provides. Not always in the way I expected, but in the way I needed. Sometimes it was through a kind word from a colleague, sometimes through an unexpected financial blessing, (you know that unexpected check in the mail) and sometimes through something as simple as a scripture that renewed my hope.

What I have learned through these experiences is that our fuel runs low when we rely on our own strength. But when we lean on God, He refills us with grace, wisdom, and endurance to keep pressing forward.

For any educator reading this who feels like they are teaching on low fuel, know this:

You are not alone. God sees you, hears you, and is walking with you. You must develop a relationship with God to withstand the struggles. Isaiah 40:31 reminds us, "But those who hope in the Lord will renew their strength. They will soar on wings like eagles; they will run and not grow weary, they will walk and not faint." Salvation and strength come through Jesus Christ. When we seek Him, He fills the empty places in our hearts.

Hopefully, this chapter has opened your eyes to the reality that teaching on low fuel is not just a metaphor—it is a real struggle. But through faith, prayer, and perseverance, we can be refueled, renewed, and restored.

A Song for The Soul

"Rock of Ages", written by Augustus Toplady in 1776:

Verse 1: Rock of Ages, cleft for me,

Let me hide myself in Thee;

Let the water and the blood,

From Thy wounded side which flowed,

Be of sin the double cure,

Save from wrath and make me pure.

Verse 2: Not the labors of my hands

Can fulfill Thy law's demands;

Could my zeal no respite know,

Could my tears forever flow,

All for sin could not atone;

Thou must save, and Thou alone.

Verse 3: Nothing in my hand I bring,

Simply to Thy cross I cling;

Naked, come to Thee for dress,

Helpless, look to Thee for grace;

Foul, I to the fountain fly,

Wash me, Savior, or I die.

Verse 4: While I draw this fleeting breath,

When mine eyes shall close in death,

When I rise to worlds unknown,

And behold Thee on Thy throne,

Rock of Ages, cleft for me,

Let me hide myself in Thee.

Chapter 2. Finding Spiritual Renewal

In this chapter, we explore how teachers can seek solace and renewal through their faith, particularly in moments of stress and burnout. This journey often requires a deep spiritual deliverance and may involve a period of waiting and patience.

Drawing on Their Faith for Spiritual Renewal During Challenging Times

Teachers can draw on their faith for spiritual renewal during challenging times by turning to the scriptures for guidance, wisdom, and encouragement. Regular engagement with scripture not only deepens their connection with God but also provides a source of strength and reassurance when facing the daily demands of the classroom. The Word serves as a reminder of their calling and purpose, helping them to navigate difficulties with grace and patience. Beyond reading scripture, prayer and meditation can offer moments of peace and clarity, allowing teachers to surrender their worries and seek divine guidance.

My sister is a testimony of how spending time in quiet reflection helps to renew her spirit, fostering a sense of resilience and hope in the face of adversity. Worship, whether through music, fellowship, or personal devotion, also plays a key role in spiritual renewal, lifting your hearts and refocusing your perspective.

Moreover, leaning on a faith-based community can provide much-needed support. Connecting with other believers—whether through church groups,

Bible studies, or fellow educators who share their faith—can serve as a source of encouragement and accountability. These connections reinforce the understanding that you are not alone in your struggles and that God is walking with you through every challenge.

As teachers, Faith reminds us that our work is not in vain and that every challenge we encounter is an opportunity for growth. It reassures us that, despite the difficulties, you are making a lasting impact on students' lives. By trusting in God's plan, teachers can find peace in knowing that "this too shall pass" and that with faith, they will emerge stronger and renewed.

Practices or Rituals Teachers Can Incorporate into Their Lives

There's an old saying that "practice makes perfect." In the same way, nurturing one's spiritual well-being requires consistent practice and intentionality. Teachers, who often give so much of themselves to their students, must also take time to replenish their own spirits. By incorporating certain faith-based practices and rituals into their daily lives, they can cultivate spiritual strength, resilience, and inner peace.

One foundational practice is regular scripture reading. Immersing oneself in God's Word provides guidance, encouragement, and wisdom, serving as a constant reminder of His presence. Meditating on scripture allows us to apply biblical principles to our work and personal lives, helping us navigate stressful situations with patience, grace, and faith.

Another powerful way to nurture spiritual well-being is through prayer and reflection. Taking a few moments each day—whether in the morning before stepping into the classroom, during lunch breaks, or in the quiet of the evening—to pray and seek God's presence can provide clarity and renewed strength. Journaling prayers or reflections on scripture can also deepen one's spiritual journey and create a tangible record of God's faithfulness over time.

Surrounding oneself with other Christian educators can also be uplifting. Engaging in faith-based groups, Bible studies, or Christian teacher organizations fosters a sense of community and accountability. These connections provide encouragement and support, reminding teachers that they are not alone in their challenges and that God is working through them in their profession.

Additionally, worship—whether through music, attending church, or participating in small-group fellowship—serves as a vital source of renewal. Worship shifts the focus from daily struggles to God's greatness, reinforcing the truth that He is in control and that all burdens can be laid at His feet.

By consistently practicing these spiritual disciplines, we not only strengthen our faith but also develop a sense of peace and confidence that can only come from God.

Their spiritual well-being is not just a private matter; it overflows into our classrooms, impacting our students, colleagues, and the overall atmosphere in which we teach. Through intentional spiritual nourishment, they are equipped to handle the pressures of their profession with a heart full of grace, patience, and unwavering faith.

Finding Solace through Faith Impacts Teachers' Ability to Cope with Stress

I believe that if we don't practice and prepare for a storm, we won't be ready when one comes. Teaching, much like life itself, is full of unexpected challenges, and without a strong spiritual foundation, it's easy to become overwhelmed by stress and burnout. That's why teachers must continually equip themselves with the full armor of God, preparing their hearts and minds for the inevitable struggles that arise in the classroom and beyond.

Ephesians 6:11 reminds us to "put on the full armor of God, so that you can take your stand against the devil's schemes." Teaching is not just a profession—it is a calling, and with that calling comes trials that can drain teachers mentally, emotionally, and spiritually.

Whether it's the weight of students' struggles, administrative pressures, or the demands of balancing work and personal life, these burdens can become overwhelming without a spiritual source of renewal.

We know that a battery drains quickly if it is never recharged. The same applies to our spirit. If we don't consistently read the Word, engage in prayer, and seek God's presence, we lack the spiritual nourishment needed to build our defense against the forces that seek to deplete us. Without that renewal, frustration, exhaustion, and discouragement can take hold, making it difficult to find joy and purpose in the work God has called us to do.

Finding solace through faith allows teachers to cope with stress and burnout by shifting their focus from the burdens of the moment to the eternal promises of God. It reminds you that you are not alone in your struggles and that your strength does not come from your own abilities but from the One who sustains them. Faith provides a source of peace in the midst of chaos, patience when challenges arise, and perseverance when the workload feels overwhelming.

Through scripture, prayer, and community with other believers, teachers can find encouragement and resilience. They are reminded that their work has meaning beyond what they see in the day-to-day, and that God is using them to make a difference in the lives of their students. By staying spiritually charged, teachers can approach each day with renewed strength, knowing that they are fully equipped to handle whatever comes their way.

Spiritual Deliverance Plays A Role

Spiritual deliverance can play a significant role in helping teachers overcome professional challenges by breaking the mental, emotional, and spiritual burdens that weigh them down. Teaching is more than just a job, it's calling, and with that calling comes pressures that can drain a teacher's spirit. The weight of student struggles, administrative expectations, lack of resources, and personal battles can create a storm of discouragement. However, just as we must put on the full armor of God to withstand spiritual warfare, teachers can seek deliverance through faith to release the burdens that threaten to overwhelm them.

Spiritual deliverance involves surrendering these challenges to God, recognizing that He alone has the power to restore, renew, and strengthen. When teachers turn to God in prayer, seeking deliverance from stress, frustration, and self-doubt, they invite Him to work in their lives, lifting the burdens that hinder their ability to serve with joy and purpose. Just as a drained battery cannot function unless recharged, a teacher who does not seek spiritual renewal will struggle to maintain resilience in the face of adversity.

I am a strong believer, through scripture, prayer, fasting, and surrounding ourselves with a faith-filled community, we can experience the freedom that comes from trusting God's plan. Deliverance brings a shift in perspective—it replaces fear with faith, exhaustion with endurance, and doubt with divine confidence. It reminds us that we are not alone, that our struggles are seen by God, and that He is always present to provide strength for the journey.

When teachers walk in spiritual deliverance, they no longer carry their challenges alone. Instead, they move forward in the knowledge that God is guiding them, equipping them, and sustaining them. This renewed strength enables them to approach their profession with peace, passion, and perseverance, no matter what obstacles arise.

Biblical Examples of Deliverance in the Midst of Challenges

One of the greatest biblical examples of deliverance is found in Exodus 14, when the Israelites stood trapped between Pharaoh's army and the Red Sea. Fear and exhaustion had set in, and they saw no way forward. But God, in His power, hallelujah, made a way where there was none—He parted the sea, delivering them from what seemed impossible. I remember years ago, my late brother Robert, told me "Only God can do the impossible." Teachers, too, can face what feels like insurmountable obstacles, but God is a deliverer. When faced with overwhelming stress, it is important to remember that, just as He made a way for the Israelites, He can make a way for teachers struggling in their profession, even when it feels impossible.

Similarly, in 2 Corinthians 12:9, Paul reminds us of God's sustaining power: "My grace is sufficient for you, for my power is made perfect in weakness." This verse speaks directly to teachers who feel weary, undervalued, or burned out. Spiritual deliverance is not about removing every hardship; it is about God's strength taking over when ours runs out. By surrendering stress and worry to Him, teachers can find peace even in difficult circumstances.

Personal Reflection: Surrendering to Deliverance

It is easy to become consumed by the daily struggles of teaching. The exhaustion, frustration, and emotional weight can feel like chains that drain the joy and passion for the profession. However, just like a drained battery cannot function unless recharged, a teacher who does not seek spiritual renewal will struggle to persevere.

There comes a moment when every teacher must ask, Am I carrying these burdens alone, or have I surrendered them to God? True deliverance happens when we recognize that we were never meant to bear the weight alone. I have personally seen teachers transformed by faith—educators who once felt trapped in burnout but found peace through prayer, fasting, and immersing themselves in God's Word. They no longer relied on their own strength but trusted that God would equip them for each day.

Practical Steps to Seek Spiritual Deliverance

Prayer and Surrender– You can start each day with a simple prayer: Lord, I surrender this day, my challenges, and my worries to You. Guide me, strengthen me, and remind me that You are in control.

Reading Scripture for Strength– Verses like Isaiah 41:10 ("Do not fear, for I am with you; do not be dismayed, for I am your God. I will strengthen you and help you.") can be a source of encouragement.

Fasting and Spiritual Renewal– Taking intentional time to seek God through fasting and reflection can break spiritual strongholds of fear, frustration, and doubt.

Seeking Community– Connecting with other faith-driven educators can provide encouragement and remind teachers that they are not alone in their struggles.

Walking in Deliverance

When you walk in spiritual deliverance, you no longer carry their challenges alone. Instead, you move forward in the knowledge that God is guiding you, equipping you, and sustaining you. This renewed strength enables you to approach your profession with peace, passion, and perseverance, no matter what obstacles arise. Just as God has delivered His people time and time again throughout history, He will continue to do so for those who trust in Him.

Benefits of Waiting Patiently for Spiritual Renewal

Waiting patiently for spiritual renewal is not always easy, especially in the fast-paced, high-pressure world of education. Teachers are often expected to give endlessly—pouring into their students, managing administrative tasks, and balancing personal responsibilities—all while feeling emotionally and spiritually drained. However, waiting on God's renewal brings profound benefits, including renewed strength, clarity, and resilience.

Renewed Strength and Endurance

Isaiah 40:31 reminds us: "But they that wait upon the Lord shall renew their strength; they shall mount up with wings as eagles; they shall run, and not be weary; and they shall walk, and not faint."

When you wait on God, rather than rushing to solve everything in their own strength, you will experience a supernatural renewal. Just as an eagle soars effortlessly rather than flapping tirelessly, teachers who rely on God's timing will find endurance even in the most demanding seasons.

Spiritual Clarity and Divine Guidance

Teachers who take time to wait on God gain clarity in decision-making. Instead of reacting out of frustration or exhaustion, they can make choices with wisdom and peace. Psalm 37:7 encourages us: "Be still before the Lord and wait patiently for Him." Waiting allows teachers to step back, pray, and seek direction rather than feeling overwhelmed by the pressures of the moment.

Inner Peace Amidst Challenges

Patience in waiting allows teachers to rest in God's promises, trusting that He is working behind the scenes even when circumstances seem unchanged. Rather than being consumed by stress, teachers can develop a deep sense of peace, knowing that God's plan is unfolding in His perfect time.

Increased Faith and Dependence on God

Waiting fosters spiritual growth. It teaches us to trust in God's provision rather than relying solely on their own efforts. The longer the wait, the stronger your faith becomes, just as Abraham waited for God's promise to be fulfilled (Romans 4:20-21).

Cultivating Patience While Waiting for Spiritual Renewal

Daily Devotion and Meditation on Scripture

Spending time in God's Word strengthens patience. Meditating on verses like Lamentations 3:25 ("The Lord is good to those who wait for

Him, to the soul who seeks Him.") reminds teachers that God rewards patience.

Practicing Gratitude in the Present

Instead of focusing on what has not yet happened, you can cultivate patience by recognizing and thanking God for small victories. Writing down daily blessings shifts focus from frustration to faith.

Engaging in Intentional Prayer and Reflection

Waiting on God requires a posture of prayer. Teachers can use prayer journals, quiet time, or even short reflective moments throughout the school day to realign their hearts with God's timing.

Surrounding Themselves with a Faith-Filled Community

Patience is easier to cultivate when teachers are surrounded by others who encourage them to trust in God's timing. Joining a Bible study, faith-based educators' group, or simply confiding in like-minded colleagues can provide strength and encouragement.

Letting Go of The Urge to Control Outcomes

Teachers often feel the need to fix every problem immediately, whether in the classroom or their personal lives. However, surrendering control and trusting that God is working—even in silence—fosters patience. Proverbs 3:5-6 encourage us to trust in the Lord rather than leaning on our own understanding.

Just as a garden takes time to bloom after seeds are planted, spiritual renewal requires patience and faith. When you wait on God, you gain strength, clarity, peace, and a deeper connection to Him. By cultivating patience through scripture, prayer, gratitude, and surrender, you allow God to work in His perfect timing, bringing renewal that sustains them through every challenge. Remembering everything is on God's timing, not ours.

Sharing Experiences of Spiritual Renewal with Colleagues

Educators can foster a spiritually supportive community by openly sharing their experiences of renewal, encouraging one another through faith, and creating spaces for collective growth. Teaching can be an isolating and overwhelming profession, but when educators come together to uplift each other spiritually, they strengthen not only themselves but also the entire teaching community.

Leading by Example Through Daily Interactions

One of the most powerful ways to share spiritual renewal is through actions. Teachers who demonstrate patience, grace, and faith in challenging situations naturally inspire their colleagues. When others witness an educator handling stress with peace and resilience, it opens the door for conversations about faith.

For example, a teacher who remains calm during a difficult staff meeting or responds to a student's behavioral challenges with compassion can later share how their time in scripture or prayer helped them maintain that composure.

Creating or Joining Faith-Based Teacher Support Groups

Educators can establish or participate in Christian-led teacher groups where they meet regularly for prayer, encouragement, and reflection. This can be as simple as:

1. A weekly devotional time before school starts.
2. A prayer group that meets in a classroom during lunch.
3. An online space where teachers share uplifting scriptures and testimonies.

Just as Matthew 18:20 reminds us, "For where two or three gather in my name, there am I with them," having a support system allows teachers to build one another up spiritually.

Encouraging Colleagues with Scripture and Testimonies

Teachers who have experienced spiritual renewal should not keep it to themselves. Sharing personal testimonies, whether through casual conversations, emails, or even a small devotion before faculty meetings—can be a source of encouragement.

For example, a teacher might say:

"Last week, I felt completely drained and overwhelmed, but spending time in Psalm 46:10—'Be still, and know that I am God'—helped me refocus. I realized that I don't have to carry everything on my own, and I just wanted to share that with you in case you need that reminder today." These small moments of sharing can plant seeds of hope in others.

Supporting Colleagues Through Prayer and Encouragement

Teachers can create a culture of encouragement by praying for and with their colleagues. When a fellow educator is struggling, simply saying, "Can I pray for you?" or sending a Bible verse can make a significant impact.

In 1 Thessalonians 5:11, we are reminded to "Encourage one another and build each other up." A simple handwritten note or message saying, "I'm praying for you today," can remind a colleague that they are not alone in their struggles.

Hosting Faith-Based Professional Development or Book Studies

Another way to share spiritual renewal is by organizing professional development sessions or book studies that incorporate faith-based themes. Books on perseverance, faith, and finding purpose in teaching can spark meaningful discussions.

Teachers can suggest books like:

1. Teach Like a Disciple: Exploring Jesus' Approach to Education
2. Fervent: A Woman's Battle Plan to Serious, Specific, and Strategic Prayer by Priscilla Shirer
3. Everyday Holy: Finding a Big God in the Little Moments by Melanie Shankle
4. Beyond the Chalkboard: A Faith Fueled Guide for Teachers by Anthony Dayse

Discussing how faith shapes their teaching journey can help teachers support each other beyond academic success.

Being a Light in the School Community

Not all teachers will be open about their faith, but that shouldn't stop educators from being a light in their workplace. As Matthew 5:16 says, "Let your light shine before others, that they may see your good deeds and glorify your Father in heaven."

By showing kindness, offering a listening ear, and uplifting colleagues, teachers can share their spiritual renewal in ways that inspire and unite their peers.

Final Thoughts

Building a spiritually supportive community among educators starts with simple, intentional acts of faith—leading by example, creating prayer groups, sharing testimonies, and offering encouragement. When teachers come together to uplift one another in their faith, they create a strong foundation of support that helps them navigate the challenges of teaching with renewed strength and purpose.

Scriptures that Provide Guidance and Comfort to Teachers?

There are numerous biblical teachings and scriptures that provide guidance, strength, and renewal for teachers navigating the challenges of their profession. Teaching can be physically, emotionally, and spiritually draining, but God's Word offers reassurance, wisdom, and encouragement to educators who seek spiritual renewal. Below are some key scriptures and teachings that can uplift and sustain teachers:

Strength for the Weary: Isaiah 40:31

"But those who hope in the Lord will renew their strength. They will soar on wings like eagles; they will run and not grow weary, they will walk and not faint."

This verse reminds teachers that when they feel exhausted and drained, placing their trust in God will provide them with renewed strength. Just as an eagle soars high above storms, teachers who rely on the Lord can rise above burnout and daily struggles.

Finding Peace in God's Presence: Philippians 4:6-7

"Do not be anxious about anything, but in every situation, by prayer and petition, with thanksgiving, present your requests to God. And the peace of God, which transcends all understanding, will guard your hearts and your minds in Christ Jesus."

Teachers often face overwhelming stress, whether from demanding workloads, student challenges, or administrative pressures. This scripture reassures educators that through prayer and surrender, they can experience God's peace, even in the most difficult situations.

Purpose in Teaching: Colossians 3:23-24

"Whatever you do, work at it with all your heart, as working for the Lord, not for human masters, since you know that you will receive an inheritance from the Lord as a reward. It is the Lord Christ you are serving."

Whenever you feel unappreciated or discouraged, this scripture serves as a reminder that your work is ultimately for God. A teacher's dedication to his/her students is an act of service, and God sees and rewards their faithfulness.

Encouragement for Tough Days: Galatians 6:9

"Let us not become weary in doing good, for at the proper time we will reap a harvest if we do not give up."

There are days when teaching feels fruitless, but this scripture encourages perseverance. Even when educators don't see immediate results, their efforts are planting seeds in students' lives that will bear fruit in time.

Wisdom in Handling Challenges: James 1:5

"If any of you lacks wisdom, you should ask God, who gives generously to all without finding fault, and it will be given to you."

Teachers often need wisdom—whether in dealing with students, managing their workload, or making decisions. This verse reassures them that they can always seek God's wisdom through prayer, and He will provide guidance.

The Armor of God: Ephesians 6:10-11

"Finally, be strong in the Lord and in his mighty power. Put on the full armor of God, so that you can take your stand against the devil's schemes."

Teaching is more than just an academic task—it is also a spiritual mission. Just as I previously mentioned the importance of being prepared for battle, this scripture reminds educators that they must equip themselves spiritually. Prayer, faith, and scripture are essential tools in standing firm against discouragement and spiritual exhaustion.

How Teachers Can Apply These Scriptures

Start the day with prayer and scripture– Reading a short devotional or a Bible verse before entering the classroom can set a positive, faith-filled tone for the day.

Memorize key scriptures– Keeping verses like Isaiah 40:31 or Philippians 4:6-7 in mind can provide strength during difficult moments.

Encourage fellow teachers– Sharing these scriptures with colleagues can build a supportive faith-based community.

Reflect on purpose– When feeling burned out, reminding oneself of Colossians 3:23-24 can reignite a sense of calling and mission in teaching.

God's Word provides an unshakable foundation for teachers seeking renewal. Whether through scriptures that offer strength, wisdom, peace, or perseverance, educators can find the encouragement they need to keep going. By staying rooted in faith and allowing scripture to guide them, teachers can continue to serve their students with renewed passion and purpose, knowing they are fulfilling God's work.

Schools and Administrators can Support Teachers

I will continue to say, teaching is not just a profession—it is a calling, one that can be both deeply rewarding and incredibly demanding. When teachers operate on "low fuel," feeling drained emotionally, physically, and spiritually, they need support from their schools and administrators to stay renewed and effective. While spiritual renewal is ultimately a personal journey, schools and administrators can play a vital role in fostering an environment that encourages faith-based resilience, reflection, and renewal.

Creating Space for Reflection and Prayer

Administrators can support teachers by providing designated quiet spaces where they can pray, meditate, or reflect during the school day. A small prayer room or a dedicated space for quiet reflection can serve as a retreat when teachers feel overwhelmed. This reinforces the idea that their spiritual well-being is valued.

Encouraging Faith-Based Support Groups

Teachers who share a common faith can benefit from faith-based teacher support groups. Administrators can encourage these groups by providing meeting spaces and allowing time for teachers to come together for prayer, scripture study, and spiritual encouragement. These groups create a sense of community and remind teachers that they are not alone in their struggles.

Offering Faith-Centered Professional Development

Schools can incorporate faith-based workshops or retreats that focus on spiritual renewal, resilience, and well-being. Sessions on balancing faith and work, overcoming burnout through prayer, or maintaining a Christ-centered perspective in teaching can help educators stay spiritually grounded.

Recognizing the Power of Purpose in Teaching

One of the most meaningful ways an administrator can support teachers is by reinforcing the purpose behind their work. Teachers who view their profession as a ministry or calling need encouragement to continue seeing it as such, even when challenges arise. Administrators can:

1. Highlight stories of teachers making a difference in students' lives.
2. Acknowledge teachers' efforts in ways that align with their faith, such as reminding them of Colossians 3:23: "Whatever you do, work at it with all your heart, as working for the Lord."
3. Encourage teachers to keep their eyes on the bigger picture rather than daily struggles.

Promoting a Culture of Encouragement and Gratitude

Spiritual renewal thrives in an environment where teachers feel appreciated. Administrators can foster this by:

1. Expressing gratitude regularly through notes, emails, or verbal affirmation.
2. Recognizing teachers' efforts in meetings or newsletters.
3. Providing opportunities for teachers to share testimonies of how their faith has helped them through challenges.

Supporting Work-Life Balance

Burnout often occurs when teachers have little time for personal renewal. Administrators can:

1. Respect teachers' time by minimizing unnecessary meetings.
2. Encourage teachers to take time for personal and spiritual reflection.
3. Advocate for fair workloads and mental health resources.

Inviting Faith Leaders to Speak and Encourage Teachers

Schools can invite pastors, chaplains, or faith-based speakers to offer encouragement to teachers. Whether through devotions, chapel services, or special events, faith leaders can provide wisdom, prayer, and support that help teachers remain spiritually strong.

Leading by Example

Administrators who demonstrate faith-based leadership, whether through their words, actions, or decisions—can inspire teachers to do the same. Leaders who model patience, kindness, and integrity create an atmosphere where faith can flourish.

Schools and administrators have the power to cultivate an environment where teachers do not have to run on "low fuel" alone. By providing spaces for reflection, encouraging faith-based support, and recognizing the deeper purpose of teaching, administrators can help educators stay spiritually renewed. When teachers are supported in their faith, they can pour more into their students and fulfill their calling with joy and strength.

As teachers navigate the challenges of their profession, seeking spiritual renewal is not just a momentary escape but an ongoing process. Through prayer, scripture, and faith-based community, they find the strength to recharge and realign with their purpose. However, renewal is not always instant—it requires patience, trust, and a willingness to surrender to God's timing.

Yet, renewal alone is not enough. Once teachers have refueled spiritually, the next step is to build resilience—the ability to withstand the storms that will inevitably come. Renewal may bring clarity and peace, but resilience ensures endurance. In the next chapter, we will explore how teachers can cultivate resilience through spiritual disciplines, mindset shifts, and a strong support system. By anchoring themselves in faith, they can stand firm, no matter what challenges arise.

A Song for The Soul

It Is Well with My Soul by Horatio Spafford (lyrics, 1873) and Philip Bliss (music, 1876)

When peace like a river, attendeth my way,

When sorrows like sea billows roll;

Whatever my lot, Thou hast taught me to say,

It is well, it is well with my soul.

Refrain:

It is well (It is well)

With my soul (With my soul),

It is well, it is well with my soul.

Chapter 3. Building Resilience

Sometimes, challenges become deeply rooted in our spirits, requiring more than a brief visit to a place of worship. Confronting these challenges with the help of the Holy Spirit and seeking support from fellow believers can be essential.

How Spiritual Practices like Prayer, Meditation, and Reflection Help Teachers

Spiritual practices like prayer, meditation, and reflection can serve as powerful tools for teachers to build resilience by fostering inner strength, emotional stability, and a renewed sense of purpose. Given the demanding nature of teaching, these practices offer ways to navigate stress, prevent burnout, and maintain a strong connection to one's faith and calling.

Prayer as a Source of Strength and Guidance

Prayer allows you to seek divine guidance and strength when facing challenges in the classroom. It serves as a moment of surrender, where you can express your struggles, frustrations, and hopes to God. By trusting in a higher power, you can release burdens that feel overwhelming and gain a renewed sense of peace. Through consistent prayer, you will cultivate patience, compassion, and perseverance, which are essential qualities for maintaining resilience in their profession.

Meditation for Mental Clarity and Emotional Stability

Teaching requires constant decision-making, adaptability, and emotional energy. Meditation helps teachers quiet their minds, center their thoughts, and regain balance. By setting aside time to meditate—whether through scripture, deep breathing, or silence. They can alleviate anxiety, increase focus, and build emotional endurance. Meditation also promotes mindfulness, helping teachers remain present and respond to challenges with calmness rather than frustration.

Reflection for Growth and Renewal

Reflection allows teachers to process their experiences, learn from their challenges, and reconnect with their purpose. Whether through journaling, scripture study, or personal contemplation, taking time for reflection fosters self-awareness and spiritual growth. It helps teachers identify what drains them and what renews them, encouraging them to set boundaries and seek the support they need.

Community Support and Shared Faith

As noted in the chapter introduction, some challenges are deeply rooted and require more than personal effort to overcome. Seeking support from fellow believers provides encouragement, wisdom, and accountability. Whether through small groups, mentorship, or faith-based discussions, teachers can find reassurance that they are not alone in their struggles. Shared faith strengthens resilience, reminding them of their higher calling and the impact of their work.

Renewed Sense of Purpose and Mission

Spiritual practices will help teachers reconnect with their purpose in education. When stress, student behavior, or administrative pressures become overwhelming, returning to their faith can remind them why they chose this path. Your work is not just about academics, it is about shaping lives, fostering growth, and serving others with love and patience.

By integrating prayer, meditation, and reflection into their daily lives, teachers can build resilience that sustains them through challenges. These practices offer a way to find peace amid chaos, strength in adversity, and renewal when they feel depleted. Through faith, they can continue their work with joy, endurance, and unwavering commitment.

The Role of Holy Spirit in Confronting Challenges

Because teachers face many challenges and how faith provides strength, the Holy Spirit plays a vital role in confronting and overcoming deeply rooted challenges by offering guidance, strength, and renewal.

Guidance and Wisdom– The Holy Spirit provides clarity in difficult situations, helping teachers discern the best course of action when faced with overwhelming challenges. As stated in John 14:26, the Holy Spirit is a counselor who teaches and reminds believers of God's truth.

Strength and Endurance– Teaching can be exhausting, both physically and emotionally. The Holy Spirit empowers educators to persevere, even when they feel drained. Isaiah 40:31 reminds us that those who hope in the Lord will renew their strength.

Peace and Comfort– Challenges in teaching can bring frustration and anxiety. The Holy Spirit provides peace that surpasses understanding (Philippians 4:7), allowing teachers to navigate struggles without being consumed by stress.

Conviction and Transformation– When you face personal or systemic obstacles, the Holy Spirit convicts you to address these challenges with faith and courage. Through prayer and reflection, you can experience transformation in their mindset and approach.

Empowerment to Make a Difference– The Holy Spirit fuels passion and resilience, equipping teachers to impact their students and communities despite hardships. Acts 1:8 speaks of the Spirit giving power to be witnesses, which applies to teachers being a light in their profession.

Finding Ongoing Support from Their Spiritual Communities

Teachers can find ongoing support from their spiritual communities when facing persistent challenges in several ways: They can tap into prayer and Intercession, Mentorship and Discipleship, Fellowship and Encouragement, service and ministry, scriptural and Devotional Resources, Accountability and Shared Struggles and Rest and Spiritual Retreats. I will elaborate on each.

Prayer and Intercession– You can lean on their faith communities for prayer support. Whether through church groups, small fellowships, or online prayer circles, knowing others are interceding for you provides strength and encouragement.

Mentorship and Discipleship– Connecting with experienced believers, pastors, or spiritual mentors offers guidance, wisdom, and reassurance. These relationships will help you navigate difficulties with biblical perspective and encouragement.

Fellowship and Encouragement– Regular gatherings with faith-based groups, such as Bible studies or teacher support groups within their churches, create a sense of belonging and renewal. Hebrews 10:25 reminds believers not to forsake assembling together for mutual encouragement.

Service and Ministry Involvement– Engaging in ministry, such as teaching Sunday school or participating in outreach programs, can help teachers find joy and perspective, reinforcing their sense of purpose beyond the classroom struggles.

Scriptural and Devotional Resources– Many spiritual communities offer devotionals, podcasts, and reading materials that provide ongoing encouragement. Immersing in these resources helps teachers remain spiritually grounded.

Accountability and Shared Struggles– Having trusted friends or accountability partners within the faith community allows teachers to share burdens, seek advice, and receive biblical wisdom in times of need.

Rest and Spiritual Retreats– Many churches and faith-based organizations offer retreats designed for teachers and professionals experiencing burnout. These provide an opportunity to step away, recharge, and reconnect with God.

Spiritual Teachings or Practices that are Effective in Building Resilience

Faith offers a wellspring of strength for teachers facing the daily challenges of the classroom. Spiritual practices provide not just relief, but renewal—helping educators persevere with a sense of divine purpose. Some of the most effective spiritual practices for resilience include:

Prayer as a Lifeline– Prayer is more than just a ritual; it is a constant dialogue with God that offers strength in moments of weakness.

When exhaustion sets in, turning to God in prayer—whether in whispered words between lessons or in deep reflection at home—provides peace that surpasses understanding (Philippians 4:6-7).

Meditating on Scripture– The Bible is filled with promises of renewal and encouragement. Reflecting on verses like Isaiah 41:10 ("Do not fear, for I am with you… I will strengthen you and help you") reminds teachers that they are never alone in their struggles.

The Power of Sabbath Rest– Teaching is an all-consuming profession, but God calls His people to rest. Setting aside intentional time to recharge—whether through observing a traditional Sabbath or simply allowing oneself to step away from work without guilt—demonstrates trust in God's provision and realigns priorities (Exodus 20:8-10).

Worship and Gratitude– Worship, whether through song, journaling, or silent reflection, shifts the focus from struggles to God's goodness.

Gratitude, even in difficult moments, changes the heart's posture, offering renewed energy and hope (1 Thessalonians 5:16-18).

Spiritual Community and Encouragement– Resilience is not meant to be built alone. Connecting with other believers—whether through church, small groups, or faith-based educator communities—provides strength, encouragement, and accountability (Hebrews 10:25).

Spiritual Practices Differ from Other Forms of Self-Care

While traditional self-care—like exercise, hobbies, or rest—helps manage stress, spiritual practices provide something deeper: a source of lasting renewal that doesn't rely on personal effort alone.

Strength from God, Not Just Self– Many self-care practices focus on what a person can do to recharge. Spiritual resilience, however, is rooted in surrender—relying on God's strength rather than one's own. As 2 Corinthians 12:9 reminds us, "My grace is sufficient for you, for my power is made perfect in weakness."

Purpose Beyond the Moment– Secular self-care can provide temporary relief, but spiritual renewal brings lasting peace and a reminder of a higher calling. When teachers ground their work in faith, challenges become opportunities for growth rather than just obstacles to overcome.

A Community of Support– Unlike individual self-care routines, faith fosters resilience through fellowship. Encouragement from fellow believers—through prayer groups, mentorship, or shared devotionals—provides a source of strength that isolation cannot.

Sustained Renewal, Not Just Relief– A vacation or a quiet evening can refresh the body, but spiritual renewal replenishes the soul. By staying connected to God, teachers find a wellspring of peace and endurance that sustains them beyond temporary fixes.

While traditional self-care is valuable, it is faith that transforms resilience from mere endurance into a deeply rooted sense of purpose and peace—allowing teachers to not just survive the challenges of their calling, but to thrive within them.

Building Resilience through Spiritual Practices

Once again, teaching is more than just a profession, it's calling. However, the weight of daily challenges can leave educators feeling drained, disheartened, and even questioning their purpose. Spiritual resilience does not erase these struggles, but it transforms how teachers respond to them.

When teachers rely on their faith for strength, they experience a deeper sense of peace, even in difficult circumstances. Spiritual practices like prayer, scripture meditation, and gratitude help reframe daily frustrations, shifting the focus from exhaustion to purpose. Teachers who cultivate resilience through faith often find greater contentment, renewed motivation, and a stronger connection to their students. Job satisfaction doesn't just come from external recognition or ideal circumstances, it grows when teachers feel grounded in something bigger than themselves.

By building spiritual resilience, educators can experience joy in their calling, not just endurance. They can move beyond surviving the demands of teaching and into a place where faith fuels their passion, making their work more meaningful and sustainable.

Incorporating Spiritual Practices into Daily Routines

Spiritual practices don't have to be time-consuming or complicated to be effective. Teachers can integrate them into their routines in simple yet powerful ways:

Start the Day with Prayer or Scripture– Even a few moments of prayer before stepping into the classroom can set the tone for the day. A scripture on a desk or written in a planner serves as a reminder of God's presence throughout the day.

Breathe and Reset– In moments of stress, pausing for a deep breath and a silent prayer can redirect anxious thoughts and bring immediate peace.

Use Transitions as Opportunities for Gratitude– While walking down the hallway or resetting between classes, teachers can take a moment to thank God for small victories—an engaged student, a kind interaction, or simply the strength to continue.

Lean on a Faith-Based Community– Finding support in a church group, online faith-based educator forums, or a trusted mentor can provide encouragement when challenges arise.

Taking time at the end of the day to reflect on moments of grace, pray over difficult situations, and surrender burdens to God helps teachers release stress instead of carrying it into the next day. Spiritual renewal does not require extra hours in an already packed schedule—it requires intentionality in turning to God during daily life.

Resources to Deepen Spiritual Practices and Build Resilience

Teachers don't have to navigate this journey alone. Many faith-based resources offer encouragement and practical guidance for incorporating spiritual resilience into daily life. Some include:

Books and Devotionals for Christian Educators– Titles like Teach Like a Disciple by Jill Miller or Awakened: Change Your Mindset to Transform Your Teaching by Angela Watson provide faith-based encouragement for teachers.

Online Communities and Podcasts– Platforms like Teach 4 the Heart and Christian Educators Association International offer blogs, podcasts, and forums where teachers can find faith-based support.

Church and Small Groups– Many churches offer prayer groups or Bible studies specifically for educators, providing a local community of encouragement.

Retreats and Conferences– Attending faith-based educator conferences or spiritual retreats can offer renewal and fresh perspective.

Daily Apps and Resources– Bible apps with devotionals for teachers, such as YouVersion, provide accessible inspiration on the go.

Seeking out these resources strengthens not only individual resilience but also fosters a sense of connection with other faith-driven educators who share the same challenges and victories.

Resilience is not built in isolation, it is cultivated through intentional spiritual practices and strengthened within a supportive community. Teaching will always present challenges, but faith equips educators to approach them with renewed strength and unwavering purpose.

While spiritual practices provide teachers with a foundation of resilience, challenges will still arise unexpectedly disruptions, difficult students, overwhelming demands. How can faith help educators navigate these difficulties without losing heart?

In the next chapter, we will explore how to face challenges head-on, applying spiritual wisdom to real-world classroom struggles. With faith as a guide, teachers can not only endure challenges but grow through them, finding grace in even the most difficult moments.

A Song for the Soul

"Amazing Grace" by John Newton (1772):

Amazing grace! How sweet the sound

That saved a wretch like me.

I once was lost, but now am found,

Was blind, but now I see.

'Twas grace that taught my heart to fear,

And grace my fears relieved;

How precious did that grace appear

The hour I first believed.

Through many dangers, toils, and snares,

I have already come;

'Tis grace hath brought me safe thus far,

And grace will lead me home.

The Lord has promised good to me,

His Word my hope secures;

He will my shield and portion be,

As long as life endures.

Yes, when this flesh and heart shall fail,

And mortal life shall cease,

I shall possess, within the veil,

A life of joy and peace.

The earth shall soon dissolve like snow,

The sun forbear to shine;

But God, who called me here below,

Will be forever mine.

Chapter 4. Navigating Challenges

In this chapter, you are offered practical advice for handling common classroom difficulties, such as challenging students, parent interactions, and administrative pressures, all from a spiritual perspective. Building a strong foundation of understanding is key, which includes recognizing and embracing the cultural diversity within the classroom. For instance, I once encountered a situation where cultural differences affected communication styles. By learning about these differences, I adapted my teaching approach to create a more inclusive environment. Additionally, establishing connections with students' parents is crucial. This goes beyond addressing behavioral issues; it involves actively celebrating their child's successes, academically and behaviorally, which helps build a collaborative partnership between home and school.

Navigating Challenges

Teachers can navigate these challenges by grounding their responses in patience, compassion, and faith. A spiritual perspective encourages educators to view difficult students not just as behavior problems but as individuals who may be struggling with unseen burdens. Responding with kindness and consistency, rather than frustration, can transform classroom dynamics.

When dealing with parents, a spirit of understanding and open communication is essential. Teachers who approach parent interactions with humility and a desire for partnership can foster trust and cooperation. Rather than engaging in conflict, they can use active listening and prayer (or moments of reflection) to seek wisdom in difficult conversations.

Administrative pressures, such as standardized testing, evaluations, and policy changes, can feel overwhelming. Teachers can lean on their faith or spiritual practices to find peace amid these demands, reminding themselves that their purpose goes beyond bureaucratic measures. Seeking support from like-minded colleagues, practicing gratitude, and setting boundaries can also help maintain balance.

Strategies Educators can Use to Understand and Embrace the Cultural Diversity

Understanding and embracing cultural diversity starts with a commitment to learning. Educators can actively educate themselves about their students' backgrounds, traditions, and communication styles. This might involve reading about different cultures, attending professional development workshops, or engaging in conversations with students and their families.

Building relationships with students is another essential strategy. By encouraging students to share their experiences, teachers validate their identities and create a classroom culture of mutual respect. Incorporating culturally relevant materials into the curriculum, such as diverse books, history lessons, and storytelling, allows students to see themselves reflected in their learning.

Another approach is fostering an open, respectful classroom environment where students feel safe expressing their identities. Establishing ground rules for respectful dialogue and encouraging curiosity about different perspectives can break down stereotypes and biases.

Adapting Teaching Approaches to Accommodate Cultural Differences

Adapting teaching methods to account for cultural differences ensures that all students feel valued and understood. For example, some cultures prioritize group collaboration over individual achievement, so incorporating cooperative learning activities can make students more comfortable. Others might emphasize respect for authority in ways that affect classroom participation, so adjusting engagement strategies (like using small-group discussions rather than calling on students directly) can be beneficial.

When students see their backgrounds and learning styles acknowledged, they are more likely to engage with the material and feel a sense of belonging. This leads to higher motivation, better academic performance, and a stronger classroom community. Inclusion is not just about accommodating differences but celebrating them, creating an environment where every student feels seen, heard, and empowered to succeed.

Ways Teachers Can Proactively Build a Collaborative Partnership

Teachers can engage with parents by initiating regular, open, and positive communication. This means reaching out not only when there is a problem but also to share good news about a child's progress. Proactive engagement can include:

Personalized Communication: Sending emails, making phone calls, or using apps to update parents on their child's academic and behavioral progress.

Parent-Teacher Conferences: Hosting structured, welcoming meetings where teachers and parents discuss student strengths and areas for growth.

Classroom Involvement: Encouraging parents to participate in activities like reading days, volunteer opportunities, or cultural celebrations.

Listening and Collaboration: Treating parents as partners by valuing their insights and working together to support the child's learning experience.

By fostering a relationship built on trust, parents and teachers can create a united front that benefits the student both at home and in the classroom.

Positive Anecdotes About Students' Achievements Strengthen The Relationship

When teachers share positive stories about students, it reassures parents that their child is valued and seen. Celebrating achievements, whether academic, social, or behavioral—creates a sense of partnership and encourages parents to be more involved in their child's learning journey.

For example, a simple note or phone call saying, "I was so proud of how your child helped a classmate today" can shift the focus from challenges to strengths. These moments build trust and foster a supportive relationship between teachers and parents, making it easier to work together when challenges do arise.

Spiritual Principles Can Help Teachers Manage Stress

Yes, spiritual principles such as patience, gratitude, compassion, and faith can help teachers stay centered and resilient. Teachers often face stressful situations, but by grounding themselves in spiritual practices, they can maintain a sense of peace and purpose.

Patience and Perspective: Viewing challenges as opportunities for growth rather than as obstacles.

Gratitude: Focusing on the positives in students and the teaching experience rather than dwelling on frustrations.

Compassion: Approaching difficult students and parents with empathy rather than judgment.

Prayer or Meditation: Taking time for personal reflection or prayer can help teachers find strength and renewal.

By incorporating these principles, teachers can create a classroom environment that is more positive, supportive, and emotionally balanced.

What resources and support systems are available to help teachers navigate these common challenges? Teachers can access several resources and support systems, including:

Professional Development: Workshops and training sessions that provide strategies for managing classroom difficulties.

Colleague Support Networks: Fellow teachers can offer advice, mentorship, and encouragement.

Faith-Based Groups: Some educators find strength in prayer groups or church communities that offer moral support.

Counselors and Mentors: Seeking guidance from experienced educators or school counselors can provide fresh perspectives.

Self-Care Practices: Engaging in activities like journaling, exercise, or quiet time to recharge.

By seeking support and continuing to learn, teachers can better navigate the pressures of their profession.

How can educators use spirituality to promote empathy and understanding in their interactions with students, parents, and colleagues? Spirituality fosters a mindset of kindness, understanding, and respect. Teachers who approach their work with a spiritual foundation can:

Lead with Empathy: By seeing students beyond their behaviors, teachers can understand the struggles they may be facing.

Encourage Respect and Inclusion: Teaching students to appreciate differences by modeling respect in all interactions.

Build Stronger Relationships: Viewing parents as allies and treating them with dignity, even in difficult conversations.

Create a Nurturing Atmosphere: Using words of encouragement and affirmations to uplift students and colleagues.

By integrating spirituality into their approach, teachers can cultivate a more compassionate and harmonious learning environment.

Teaching comes with its share of challenges—difficult students, demanding parents, and administrative pressures. However, by embracing a spiritual perspective, teachers can navigate these obstacles with patience, empathy, and faith. Recognizing and respecting cultural diversity, fostering strong partnerships with parents, and adapting teaching methods to create an inclusive classroom all contribute to a more supportive and enriching educational environment.

Yet even the most dedicated educators cannot sustain this journey alone. Just as students thrive in a classroom built on connection and understanding, teachers, too, need a strong support system. The pressures of teaching can feel overwhelming, but through faith and a sense of community, educators can find renewal and strength.

As we move into the next chapter, we'll explore the importance of building a support network within the teaching profession. How can teachers uplift one another? What role does faith play in strengthening these connections? And how can a sense of community provide the encouragement and resilience needed to sustain a meaningful teaching career? Let's dive deeper into the power of community in Chapter 5.

<u>A Song for the Soul</u>

What a Friend We Have in Jesus" by Joseph M. Scriven (lyrics, 1855) and Charles C. Converse (music, 1868). This timeless hymn speaks to taking burdens and challenges to God in prayer, offering a spiritual anchor for teachers dealing with classroom difficulties and pressures.

Here's the first verse and refrain:

What a Friend We Have in Jesus

What a friend we have in Jesus,

All our sins and griefs to bear!

What a privilege to carry

Everything to God in prayer!

Oh, what peace we often forfeit,

Oh, what needless pain we bear,

All because we do not carry

Everything to God in prayer!

Chapter 5. Community Support

In this chapter, we stress the importance of community and support networks within the teaching profession, and how these connections can be strengthened through faith.

In the demanding world of education, no teacher is an island. The strength to navigate challenges often comes from the community around us—our colleagues, mentors, and even the families we serve. For many, faith serves as the anchor that binds these relationships, offering a shared purpose and a source of renewal. In this chapter, we'll explore the essential role of community in the teaching profession and how these connections can be deepened through shared faith and mutual support.

Questions to Ask Yourself

Reflective Questions for Teachers:

Who are the key people in your support network, and how have they helped you in your teaching journey?

_____

_____

_____

_____

_____

_____

_____

_____

_____

How has your faith influenced the way you build relationships with colleagues and students?

_____

_____

_____

_____

_____

_____

_____

_____

_____

What steps could you take to strengthen your sense of community within your school?

_____

_____

_____

_____

_____

_____

_____

_____

_____

Using Your Faith to Support One Another in Times of Stress or Burnout

Faith can be a powerful source of renewal and strength for teachers, especially during challenging times. One-way teachers can support one another through shared prayer or moments of reflection, creating a space where they can encourage each other spiritually. Faith also teaches principles of compassion, patience, and grace—reminding teachers to extend kindness not only to their students but also to their colleagues who may be struggling.

Additionally, faith-centered support groups within schools can provide a safe space for teachers to share burdens, offer words of encouragement, and uplift one another through scripture, devotionals, or faith-based discussions. Acts of service, such as leaving a thoughtful note, checking in on a colleague, or simply offering to help with a task, are small but meaningful ways teachers can put their faith into action to combat burnout. When teachers anchor themselves in faith and extend that support to one another, they foster a workplace environment that is filled with strength, hope, and resilience.

The Community Plays a Role Too

The broader community plays a crucial role in sustaining teachers by providing resources, encouragement, and partnership. Parents can support teachers not only by being involved in their child's education but also by recognizing the hard work and dedication of educators. Simple gestures, such as expressing gratitude, volunteering in the classroom, or advocating for teachers' needs, help create a more supportive school environment.

Local organizations, including churches, businesses, and nonprofits, can also play a vital role by offering mentorship programs, providing classroom supplies, or sponsoring initiatives that support teacher well-being. Faith-based communities can extend their support through prayer groups, appreciation events, or even offering mental health and wellness resources for educators.

To strengthen these connections, schools can foster open communication between teachers and community members through regular meetings, outreach programs, and collaborative initiatives. Creating mentorship opportunities where teachers are paired with community leaders or forming partnerships with local organizations for professional development and wellness programs can also deepen this support system. When teachers feel valued and backed by their community, it strengthens their sense of purpose and helps prevent burnout.

Teaching can often feel like running on low fuel—giving so much of yourself to your students, managing daily challenges, and striving to meet endless expectations. Without the right support, it's easy to feel drained, isolated, and on the verge of burnout. But the truth is, no teacher is meant to navigate this journey alone.

The strength to keep going comes from the relationships we build—with colleagues who understand our struggles, mentors who guide us, and families who support the work we do. When we lean on these connections, we refill our tanks, finding encouragement, wisdom, and a renewed sense of purpose.

Faith, too, serves as a vital source of renewal. It reminds us why we do this work, helping us see beyond the stress and into the deeper impact we are making. When teachers come together in faith—through prayer, shared encouragement, or simply uplifting one another in moments of struggle—they create a strong, supportive community that sustains them.

Teaching on low fuel is unsustainable, but through faith and community, we find the strength to keep going. By investing in our support networks and embracing the power of shared faith, we ensure that our passion for teaching doesn't run dry. Instead of just surviving, we thrive—bringing light, energy, and purpose to the work we are called to do.

As we move forward, let's commit to refueling ourselves and each other. Because when teachers support one another, they don't just endure the challenges of teaching—they rise above them, stronger and more resilient than before.

A Song for The Soul

A wonderful gospel song for Chapter 5, "Community Support," is "Blest Be the Tie That Binds" by John Fawcett (lyrics, 1782) and Johann G. Nägeli (music, 1820). This hymn celebrates the strength of Christian fellowship and the bonds of love and support within a community, making it a perfect fit for a chapter about building and nurturing supportive networks through faith.

Here's the first verse:

Blest Be the Tie That Binds

Blest be the tie that binds

Our hearts in Christian love;

The fellowship of kindred minds

Is like to that above.

Chapter 6. Personal Growth

In this chapter, we encourage all to have personal growth and self-care practices that align with spiritual principles, emphasizing the importance of prioritizing one's well-being.

In the fast-paced and often overwhelming world of education, it's easy to lose sight of the most important relationship you have—the one with yourself. Personal growth is not a luxury; it's a necessity for teachers who wish to thrive rather than just survive. Rooted in spiritual principles, self-care becomes more than just a practice; it's a way to honor your purpose and calling. In this chapter, we'll explore how prioritizing your well-being can unlock your potential, deepen your faith, and transform your teaching.

Questions to Ask Yourself

Reflective Questions for teachers:

What does personal growth mean to you, and how has it impacted your teaching or daily life?

_____

_____

_____

_____

_____

_____

How does neglecting self-care affect your ability to teach and connect with others?

_____

_____

_____

_____

_____

_____

In what ways do spiritual principles guide your approach to self-care and growth?

_____

_____

_____

_____

_____

_____

Application Questions:

What self-care practices could you incorporate into your routine to align with your spiritual values?

_____

_____

_____

_____

_____

_____

How can setting boundaries and prioritizing your well-being benefit your students and colleagues?

_____

_____

_____

_____

_____

_____

What steps can you take to create a personal growth plan that includes reflection, prayer, or meditation?

_____

_____

_____

_____

_____

_____

Personal Growth and Its Contribution

Personal growth enables teachers to lead with wisdom, patience, and a sense of purpose. The more we invest in our own learning, emotional well-being, and spiritual development, the better we can serve our students. Growth fosters resilience, helping us navigate the challenges of the classroom with confidence instead of frustration. It also keeps our passion for teaching alive, ensuring that we don't become stagnant or discouraged. By prioritizing self-improvement—through continued education, self-reflection, and faith-based practices—we cultivate a mindset that sees challenges as opportunities rather than obstacles.

Fostering Self-Care and Personal Development

Teaching is not meant to be a solitary journey. Educators thrive when they lean on one another for encouragement, wisdom, and accountability. Colleagues can support each other by sharing self-care strategies, encouraging work-life balance, and offering a listening ear in difficult moments. Whether through mentorship, prayer groups, or simple acts of kindness, educators can help each other maintain a sense of joy and purpose in their work. A culture of support reminds us that we are not alone and that our well-being matters just as much as the success of our students.

Providing Faith through Guidance and Reassurance

There are seasons in every teacher's journey when progress feels slow, and growth feels out of reach. It is in these moments that faith becomes a guiding force. Faith reassures us that our work has purpose, even when results aren't immediate. It reminds us to trust in God's timing, to be patient with ourselves, and to find strength beyond our own limitations. Prayer, scripture, and reflection can help educators stay grounded, reminding them that their growth—though sometimes invisible—is unfolding according to a greater plan.

Throughout this chapter, we have explored the importance of personal growth in the life of an educator. Teaching is more than delivering lessons; it is an ongoing journey of self-discovery, renewal, and perseverance.

When teachers neglect their own development—emotionally, spiritually, and professionally—they risk running on empty, struggling to pour into their students from a depleted source. As we conclude this chapter, let's reflect on three essential questions that highlight the role of personal growth in building a fulfilling teaching career.

At the beginning of this book, we acknowledged the exhaustion that often accompanies the teaching profession. Running on low fuel—physically, emotionally, and spiritually—can make it difficult to find joy and fulfillment in our work. Personal growth is not just about professional development; it is about replenishing our spirits so that we can serve with passion rather than burnout.

This naturally leads us to the next chapter: Integration of Faith and Teaching. As we grow personally and spiritually, our faith becomes more than a source of encouragement, it becomes the foundation of how we teach, lead, and impact the lives of our students. In the next chapter, we will explore how faith and teaching are not separate but deeply intertwined. When faith is fully integrated into the classroom, it transforms our perspective, strengthens our resilience, and allows us to teach with purpose and conviction.

A Song for The Soul

A great gospel song for Chapter 6, "Personal Growth," is "Higher Ground" by Johnson Oatman Jr. (lyrics, 1898) and Charles H. Gabriel (music, 1898). This hymn reflects a desire for spiritual growth, personal development, and striving for a closer relationship with God, aligning beautifully with the themes of self-care and prioritizing well-being.

Here's the first verse and refrain:

I'm pressing on the upward way,

New heights I'm gaining every day;

Still praying as I onward bound,

"Lord, plant my feet on higher ground."

Refrain:

Lord, lift me up and let me stand,

By faith, on Heaven's tableland,

A higher plane than I have found;

Lord, plant my feet on higher ground

Chapter 7. Integration of Faith and Teaching

In this chapter, we discuss how teachers can integrate their faith into their teaching practice, creating a more holistic and meaningful experience for both them and their students.

Teaching is more than imparting knowledge, it's about shaping lives and cultivating hearts. For teachers of faith, this journey is enriched by the opportunity to bring spiritual principles into their work. Integrating faith into teaching practice creates a deeper sense of purpose, guiding interactions and decisions in ways that resonate with both students and educators. In this chapter, we'll explore practical and meaningful ways to weave faith into your teaching, creating a holistic experience that uplifts and inspires.

Reflective Statements:

The ways faith influenced my view as a teacher

My faith is the foundation of my teaching journey, shaping the way I approach my students, my classroom, and the challenges that come with this calling. Through my walk with God, my life experiences, and the mentors who have guided me, I have come to see teaching as more than just a profession—it is a ministry, a sacred opportunity to impact lives in meaningful ways.

Having a relationship with God transforms my perspective. It allows me to see my students not just through my own eyes but through His—recognizing their potential, their struggles, and their need for encouragement. Faith teaches me to extend grace, patience, and understanding, even in difficult moments. Instead of reacting to challenges with frustration, I strive to approach them with wisdom and compassion, knowing that every interaction can leave a lasting impression.

I believe that teaching, much like preaching, is a calling. God entrusts teachers with the responsibility of shaping minds and hearts, and this assurance strengthens me on the hard days. When my energy is depleted and my "fuel gets low," I am reminded that I am not alone—God walks beside me, providing the strength, guidance, and renewal I need to continue. My faith reassures me that every lesson taught, every word of encouragement, and every act of kindness is part of a greater purpose.

Ultimately, my faith allows me to teach with love, integrity, and a sense of mission. It is the quiet strength behind my patience, the wisdom behind my words, and the peace in knowing that even on the most challenging days, I am doing the work I was called to do.

Challenges in Integrating Faith into My Teaching Practice

One of the greatest challenges I face when integrating faith into my teaching is navigating the tension between what is right and what is wrong in an environment where faith is not always openly embraced. I can begin my day with a heart full of purpose, ready to create a positive and meaningful experience for my students—one where they feel seen, valued, and inspired. However, the realities of the classroom, the unexpected struggles, and the distractions of daily challenges can sometimes pull me away from my original intentions.

There are moments when frustration, negativity, or conflict try to overshadow the peace I strive to bring into my teaching. Even with prayer, these challenges can be difficult to navigate. The enemy works in subtle ways—through discouragement, setbacks, and moments of exhaustion. But in those moments, I remind myself of God's promise: He will never leave me nor forsake me, even when I feel backed into a corner.

Integrating faith into my teaching does not mean that every day will be perfect or that I won't face obstacles. Instead, it means leaning into God's strength when my own is depleted, extending grace when patience wears thin, and remembering that even on the hardest days, I am called to this work for a reason. Faith is not just about speaking words of encouragement; it is about living them, even in adversity. And that is where true faith in teaching is tested and strengthened.

Inspiring Students Through Faith Without Imposing on Their Beliefs

Faith is not just about words, it is about how we live, how we treat others, and how we approach challenges. As a teacher, I strive to let my faith shine through my actions, creating an environment of kindness, integrity, and encouragement without imposing my beliefs on my students.

One way I do this is by leading with love and compassion. By demonstrating patience, understanding, and a willingness to listen, I model values that resonate universally—respect, perseverance, and grace. These are not exclusive to any one faith; they are principles that help build character and foster a supportive learning environment.

Additionally, I inspire students by encouraging them to reflect on their own values, purpose, and sense of meaning. I created a classroom where all perspectives are honored, where students feel safe to express themselves, and where mutual respect is the foundation. Rather than preaching faith, I aim to embody it—showing resilience in adversity, gratitude in success, and humility in leadership.

Ultimately, my goal is to uplift and empower students through the principles of faith—without telling them what to believe, but by showing them the power of kindness, hope, and perseverance in action.

Incorporating Spiritual Principles into the Classroom

Faith is not just something I practice outside of work, it is the foundation of how I teach, interact, and lead in my classroom. One of the most practical ways I integrate spiritual principles like kindness, patience, and empathy is by being intentional in my words and actions. I strive to create a classroom environment where every student feels valued, respected, and supported. This means practicing active listening, showing grace when mistakes are made, and encouraging students to treat one another with respect and understanding. Simple gestures, such as greeting students warmly, offering words of encouragement, and taking the time to understand their struggles, help reinforce these principles daily.

Faith as a Guide in Difficult Situations

Challenges in the classroom are inevitable—whether it's conflict between students, a struggling learner, or my own moments of frustration. In these situations, my faith reminds me to pause, pray, and seek wisdom before reacting. Conflict resolution, for example, requires patience, discernment, and fairness—qualities that faith strengthens within me. Instead of responding with frustration, I ask myself, "How would God want me to handle this?" I focus on leading with grace, finding solutions that promote growth rather than division. When students struggle, I remind them (and myself) that setbacks are not the end of the story. My faith helps me offer encouragement, reminding them that perseverance, resilience, and self-belief can lead to breakthroughs

Modeling Faith-Based Values in Daily Interactions

The most powerful way to share faith is through example. I may not always speak openly about faith in my professional setting, but I can demonstrate it through my actions. Whether it's showing patience with a challenging student, maintaining integrity in difficult moments, or uplifting a discouraged colleague, I strive to reflect the love and grace that faith teaches. I want my students and colleagues to see that faith isn't just something spoken—it's something lived. By maintaining a spirit of kindness, humility, and encouragement, I hope to leave a lasting impact that extends beyond the classroom.

Reflective Statements:

The Impact of Faith on Teaching and Learning

Integrating faith into teaching creates a deeper sense of purpose for both students and educators. For teachers, faith serves as a guiding force, shaping their approach to instruction, discipline, and student engagement. It reminds us that our role extends beyond academics—we are also nurturing character, resilience, and emotional well-being. For students, faith-driven values such as kindness, patience, and empathy create a classroom atmosphere where they feel supported, encouraged, and valued. When a teacher models these principles, it inspires students to develop their own sense of integrity, purpose, and compassion, making the learning experience more meaningful for all.

The Role of School Culture and Policy in Faith Integration

A school's culture and policies play a crucial role in either supporting or challenging the integration of faith into teaching. Some schools embrace faith-based principles as part of their mission, making it easier for teachers to openly incorporate spiritual values into their instruction. Others may have policies that restrict direct expressions of faith, requiring teachers to find more subtle ways to model their beliefs through actions rather than words. Regardless of the setting, faith can still be present through the way teachers treat students, handle conflicts, and create a nurturing environment. In schools where faith integration is more challenging, teachers must be especially mindful of maintaining respect for diverse beliefs while staying true to their values.

Collaboration Among Teachers of Different Faith Backgrounds

Teachers of different faith backgrounds can work together to create a respectful and inclusive environment by focusing on shared values rather than differences. Kindness, respect, integrity, and empathy are principles that transcend religious boundaries and can be embraced by all educators. Open dialogue, mutual respect, and a commitment to understanding each other's perspectives help foster collaboration. By recognizing that faith, in its many forms, can be a source of strength and guidance, teachers can support one another in uplifting their students while maintaining a culture of inclusivity and respect.

A Song for The Soul

A well-known gospel song that works beautifully for Chapter 7, "Integration of Faith and Teaching," is "This Little Light of Mine" (lyrics, traditional, first published in 1920s). While it's a bit newer than some of the others, it remains widely recognized and carries a strong message about letting one's light (faith) shine in all aspects of life.

Here's the first verse:

This little light of mine, I'm gonna let it shine,

This little light of mine, I'm gonna let it shine,

This little light of mine, I'm gonna let it shine,

Let it shine, let it shine, let it shine.

This song is about sharing your light (or faith) with the world, which aligns with the idea of integrating faith into teaching and positively influencing others.

Chapter 8 Finding Purpose

In this chapter, we look at ways we can help teachers rediscover their sense of purpose and passion for teaching by connecting it to their spiritual beliefs and values.

Teaching is a calling, but even the most dedicated educators can sometimes feel disconnected from the passion that first brought them to the profession. The day-to-day pressures of teaching can cloud that sense of purpose, leaving many wondering why they started in the first place. Yet, by reconnecting with their spiritual beliefs and values, teachers can rediscover the deeper meaning behind their work. In this chapter, we'll explore how spiritual reflection, and alignment can help educators find renewed purpose and joy in their journey."

Inspirations

I was initially inspired to pursue teaching because of my deep desire to make a difference in students' lives. The idea of shaping young minds, fostering curiosity, and helping students realize their potential was incredibly motivating. Over time, however, the daily demands of teaching—lesson planning, grading, administrative tasks, and other challenges—sometimes made it difficult to stay connected to that original passion. But as I have grown in my career, I've come to see teaching not just as a job but as a calling—an opportunity to serve, uplift, and guide students beyond academics. My sense of purpose has evolved from simply wanting to educate to understanding the importance of being a mentor, encourager, and source of inspiration.

Experiencing Moments of Feeling Disconnected

There have been moments when the pressures of teaching made me feel disconnected from my passion. The overwhelming workload, challenging student behaviors, and feeling underappreciated at times have made me question my purpose. However, what brought me back was taking time for self-reflection, reconnecting with my "why," and remembering the impact I've had on students. Seeing former students succeed, receiving heartfelt notes of appreciation, and reminding myself that teaching is about more than just content delivery—it's about shaping lives—has helped reignite my passion. Additionally, leaning on my faith and seeking spiritual renewal through prayer and reflection has given me the strength and motivation to keep going.

Spiritual Beliefs Do Influence

My spiritual beliefs deeply influence my view of teaching as a calling. I see it as a way to serve others, to be a light in my students' lives, and to demonstrate patience, kindness, and compassion. I believe that every student is unique and has a purpose, and part of my role as a teacher is to help them discover their potential. Teaching, for me, is an act of love and service, and my faith reminds me that my work has a greater meaning beyond just academics—it's about nurturing hearts and minds. When I focus on teaching as a spiritual calling, it gives me the strength to persevere, even in difficult moments.

Practices That Could Help You Stay Connected

Staying connected to my sense of purpose in teaching requires intentional practices that nourish both my mind and spirit. Daily, I can begin with a moment of prayer or meditation, setting an intention for the day and asking for patience, wisdom, and strength. Journaling about meaningful moments in the classroom—whether a student's breakthrough, a heartfelt conversation, or a small victory—can serve as a reminder of why I teach. Weekly, I can engage in professional reflection by revisiting my "why" and reading inspiring books or scriptures that reinforce my purpose. Connecting with a supportive community of fellow educators, either through discussions or faith-based groups, can also provide encouragement and renewal.

Reflecting on Your Spiritual Values

Teaching comes with inevitable challenges—difficult students, demanding workloads, and moments of doubt. Reflecting on my spiritual values reminds me that my work has a greater purpose and that I am not alone in my struggles. My faith teaches patience, perseverance, and grace, which are essential in overcoming discouragement. When faced with a challenge, I can turn to prayer, scripture, or quiet reflection to regain perspective. Trusting that every difficulty is an opportunity for growth helps me approach challenges with a sense of peace rather than frustration. My spiritual values also encourage me to show love and kindness, even in the most trying situations, keeping me grounded in my purpose.

Steps in Aligning Your Teaching Practices

To align my teaching practices with my core beliefs and values, I must be intentional about the way I interact with students, colleagues, and my work. First, I can ensure that my classroom environment reflects the values of respect, compassion, and encouragement, fostering a space where students feel seen and valued. Second, I can incorporate moments of gratitude and reflection into my teaching routine, reminding myself and my students of the importance of growth and learning beyond academics. Lastly, I can make a conscious effort to lead by example—demonstrating patience, kindness, and integrity in all that I do. Seeking professional development that aligns with my values and finding mentors who share a similar approach to teaching can further reinforce this alignment.

The Benefits of a Strong Sense of Purpose

A strong sense of purpose serves as an anchor for teachers, helping them stay motivated, resilient, and passionate about their work despite the challenges they face. When teachers have a clear understanding of why they teach, they bring more energy, creativity, and patience into the classroom. This directly benefits students by fostering a more engaging and supportive learning environment. Students thrive when they feel their teacher genuinely cares about their growth, both academically and personally. A purpose-driven teacher also models perseverance and dedication, inspiring students to pursue their own goals with confidence.

Roles of The Support Networks, and Spiritual Communities

Teaching can often feel isolating, especially when faced with stress, exhaustion, or discouragement. Support networks, whether they include colleagues, friends, mentors, or faith-based communities, provide teachers with encouragement, wisdom, and a sense of belonging. Spiritual communities, in particular, offer a source of strength, reminding educators that their work is part of a greater purpose. Through shared faith, prayer, reflection, and uplifting conversations, teachers can find renewed inspiration and reassurance. Having a strong support system allows educators to navigate difficulties with resilience and maintain their passion for teaching.

Creating An Environment that Encourages Personal Values and Beliefs

Schools can foster an environment that supports teachers' personal values and beliefs by promoting a culture of respect, reflection, and open dialogue. Providing professional development opportunities focused on purpose-driven teaching, self-care, and well-being can help educators reconnect with their passion. Creating mentorship programs and teacher support groups allows educators to share experiences and uplift one another. Schools can also encourage moments of reflection, whether through mindful practices, quiet spaces, or faculty discussions that acknowledge the deeper impact of teaching. When teachers feel valued and supported in aligning their work with their core beliefs, they are more likely to stay engaged, fulfilled, and effective in their roles.

A Song for The Soul

Blessed Assurance" by Fanny J. Crosby (lyrics, 1873) and Phoebe P. Knapp (music, 1873). This hymn is a powerful expression of faith, confidence, and purpose, making it a fitting song for a chapter on rediscovering purpose and passion through spiritual beliefs.

Here's the first verse:

Blessed assurance, Jesus is mine!

Oh, what a foretaste of glory divine!

Heir of salvation, purchase of God,

Born of His Spirit, washed in His blood.

The song's theme of assurance and confidence in God's purpose resonates deeply with finding and living out one's purpose.

Friends, throughout this book, I have explored how teaching on low fuel can take a toll on your mental, physical, emotional, and—most importantly—spiritual well-being. The demands of the classroom can be overwhelming, leaving many educators feeling exhausted and discouraged. However, I have also shown that there is hope. No matter how empty your tank may feel, Jesus is the ultimate source of renewal.

By embracing faith, prayer, and spiritual practices, you can build resilience, navigate challenges, and find strength in your community. Each chapter has offered strategies to help you refuel—whether through personal growth, support networks, or integrating faith into your teaching. But above all, the most powerful resource you have is the Holy Spirit. If you seek His guidance, He will lead you, strengthen you, and equip you for the journey ahead.

As mentioned, numerous times throughout the book, "teaching is more than a profession; it is a calling". And when you lean on your faith, you will not only endure the challenges but also find renewed passion and purpose in your work. May you walk forward with confidence, knowing that you are never alone on this journey. The One who called you will sustain you. Continue to stay fueled with the word of God.... Until Next time....

"But those who hope in the Lord will renew their strength. They will soar on wings like eagles; they will run and not grow weary, they will walk and not be faint." — Isaiah 40:31

Music References

Newton, J. (1772). Amazing grace [Hymn].

Crosby, F. J. (1873). Blessed assurance (P. P. Knapp, Music) [Hymn].

Fawcett, J. (1782). Blest be the tie that binds (J. G. Nägeli, Music) [Hymn].

Oatman, J. Jr. (1898). Higher ground (C. H. Gabriel, Music) [Hymn].

Spafford, H. (1873). It is well with my soul (P. Bliss, Music) [Hymn].

Traditional. (1920s). This little light of mine [Hymn].

Scriven, J. M. (1855). What a friend we have in Jesus (C. C. Converse, Music) [Hymn].

Bible References

New International Version. (2011). Holy Bible, New International Version. Zondervan.

King James Bible. (1769/2017). Holy Bible, King James Version. Cambridge University Press.

Article Reference

Agyapong, B., Obuobi-Donkor, G., Burback, L., & Wei, Y. (2022). Stress, burnout, anxiety and depression among teachers: A scoping review. International Journal of Environmental Research and Public Health, 19(17), 10706. https://doi.org/10.3390/ijerph191710706

About the Author

Dr. Anthony Dayse is an experienced educator, author, and advocate for teacher well-being. With a deep passion for both education and faith, Dr. Dayse has dedicated his career to supporting teachers who feel overwhelmed and exhausted by the demands of the profession. Drawing from 30 plus years of classroom experience, as well as personal and spiritual insights, he provides practical strategies to help educators find renewal, resilience, and purpose in their work.

As the author of Beyond the Chalkboard and A Teacher's Nightmare, Dr. Dayse sheds light on the real struggles teachers face daily. A Teacher's Nightmare draws from personal experiences—both his own and those of many educators—highlighting the challenges, frustrations, and triumphs that come with the profession. Through storytelling, reflection, and faith-based encouragement, his work serves as a guide for teachers seeking to navigate the highs and lows of their calling.

Acknowledgment

To my beloved parents, Harold Dayse, Sr. and Sarah J. Dayse, who now watch over me from heaven—thank you for the unwavering love, wisdom, and guidance you instilled in me. Your strength and faith shaped the man I am today, and though you are no longer here in body, your spirit remains my guiding light. When my fuel runs low, I remember the lessons you taught me and look to the hills, knowing that my help comes from above. Your legacy lives on in every step I take.

-Anthony

www.ingramcontent.com/pod-product-compliance
Lightning Source LLC
Chambersburg PA
CBHW061656120626
46550CB00003B/968